BLUE PETER SPECIAL ASSIGNMENT

London, Amsterdam and Edinburgh

Blue Peter Special Assignment

LONDON:	Film Cameraman	Ian Hilton
	Sound Recordist	Richard Boulter
	Director	Peter Ridsdale Scott

AMSTERDAM:	Film Cameraman	David Jackson
	Sound Recordist	Dennis Cartwright
	Director	David Brown

EDINBURGH:	Film Cameraman	Eugene Carr
	Sound Recordist	Ron Blight
	Director	David Turnbull

| | Research by | Dorothy Smith |
| | Producer | Edward Barnes |

BLUE PETER
SPECIAL ASSIGNMENT

London, Amsterdam and Edinburgh

EDWARD BARNES AND DOROTHY SMITH

---

*With eighteen full colour photographs and with
line drawings by Margaret Power*

A Piccolo Original

PAN BOOKS LTD
LONDON

First published 1973 by Pan Books Ltd,
33 Tothill Street, London, SW1
by arrangement with the British Broadcasting
Corporation.

ISBN 0 330 23480 3

The stories for this volume have been based on
film scripts by Peter Ridsdale Scott, David Brown
and David Turnbull
The cover photograph for this volume is by John Howarth
Other photographs by Dennis Cartwright, John Howarth
and Ken Looms

The photograph of the Edinburgh
Military Tattoo is reproduced by
courtesy of The Edinburgh Military
Tattoo Committee, those of Edinburgh
Old Town and the Scott Monument by
courtesy of the British Tourist Authority.

Also available in Piccolo
BLUE PETER SPECIAL ASSIGNMENT: *Stories from
Rome, Paris and Vienna* by Edward Barnes & Dorothy Smith

*Made and printed in Great Britain by
Cox & Wyman Ltd, London, Reading and Fakenham*

HELLO THERE!

Every year I've been on Blue Peter, something unexpected and different has turned up just when I was least expecting it.

For instance, two years ago I suddenly found myself on an aeroplane of the Queen's Flight, heading for East Africa with Princess Anne.

Last year when I was busy working on our Christmas programme, I was asked if I would like to set off as a Roving Reporter on six Blue Peter Special Assignments. The locations were to be six different capital cities of Europe, and the assignments were to find out all about what is going on in the cities today, and to discover some of the real-life tales of the past that made each particular city great.

As my favourite things have always been travel, meeting people and investigating true stories, I leapt at the chance. This book tells the stories of three of the films we made, and some of the peculiar behind-the-scene events that always seem to happen when I'm out with Blue Peter Cameras.

If you live in Edinburgh or London you might find there are some things about your own home town that you didn't know before. I've lived in London all my life, but I learned a lot about it when I was there on Special Assignment. Someone once wrote a travel book called 'Surprising Amsterdam' and that's just what it is: so near to Britain – in many ways so like home – and yet so different. Surprising in fact!

Valerie Singleton

THE CITY OF LONDON

I arrived at the City of London, with the Blue Peter cameras, at seven-thirty in the morning, on a hydrofoil bringing the first of a whole army of workers to their jobs in the banks, offices and markets of the City of London. Every morning, thousands and thousands of men and women leave their homes and travel to the City – by train, by underground, by bus, by car, even on bicycles and on foot. The hydrofoil is the very latest way of getting to work, it rises out of the water on stream-lined fins or foils and can travel at speeds of 50 knots, but as it cuts through the water on its way up from Greenwich, it uses the oldest means of travel in London – the River Thames.

Around me what has been called the richest square mile in the world got ready to begin the business of the new day. But behind that familiar skyline with the Tower and St Paul's the City retained an air of mystery . . . and even though I'm a Londoner, in the City I feel almost a stranger.

The low fast modern boat was a tiny white speck against the great grey span of Tower Bridge, the last bridge between the City and the sea. It was opened in 1894, because Londoners needed a bridge which would take traffic across the Thames but also open to allow the tall ships to go through to discharge their cargoes up the river.

By Act of Parliament, river traffic takes precedence over road traffic. Any hour of the day or night the bridge must be opened for any ship that makes the right signals – a ball and pennant at the mast by day, and two red lights at the mast by night. The traffic that thunders over Tower Bridge gets heavier every day, whilst the tall ships that steam into the Upper Pool get fewer and fewer. Most of the docks above the bridge have closed down now, so the Royal Navy, making courtesy calls to the City, is practically the only customer left.

Tower Bridge

A few years ago the bridge would open seven or eight times a day. Now it often remains closed all week. But every Sunday, at 8.30 AM, road traffic is stopped, the gigantic cog-wheels begin to turn, and the huge arms of the bridge are raised – just to show that Tower Bridge, which has never failed in eighty-six years, is still in working order.

A hill, a river and a good cross-over point are key factors in the siting of a city for defence and access and trade. In fact, the very name London is derived from the Celtic Llyn-dyn, which means a fortified emplacement by water. The high ground of Ludgate Hill would have been an ideal site for such a settlement, protected on the South by the river, and by vast forests to the North.

The Romans in their turn recognized the advantages of this site as a port for overseas trade. They built a wall round the settlement and called it Londinium. Parts of the old London Wall can still be seen today in the churchyard of All Hallows, London Wall. After the Romans left Britain in AD 410 very little development happened until the time of the Saxon King, Alfred the Great. He rebuilt the city wall and revived trade – but perhaps most important of all he appointed a government and made London the capital city of his kingdom.

From this time the City grew in importance and William the Conqueror in his turn built the White Tower, part of the Tower of London, to guard the powerful and turbulent City. For nearly 900 years the Tower has been used as a fortress, a palace, a treasure house, a prison and a place of execution.

Tower Green looks so calm and beautiful today; it is

The Tower

very hard to believe that it was once the scene of bloody executions. It was here that the most important people – enemies of the monarch and the state – were executed. Ordinary criminals whose deaths meant little to the state met their end beyond the walls, and in public, on Tower Hill. But those who died here, quietly and privately, were people whose executions might have caused riot and revolution. The deathroll is impressive: Queen Anne Boleyn, Margaret Countess of Salisbury, Queen Catherine Howard, Jane, Viscountess of Rochford, Lady Jane Grey.

Lady Jane Grey's story is probably the saddest of them all. She was seventeen years old and had harmed no one. But she was a cousin of King Edward VI and when he died her ambitious father-in-law declared her Queen of England. On June 10th, 1553, she was received in state at the Tower. Clad in royal robes and presented with the Crown Jewels her accession was proclaimed from the corners of the fortress.

But Queen Mary, elder sister of the dead King Edward, had a stronger claim to the throne, and after a successful uprising Jane was declared a usurper and sentenced to death. She had been Queen for only nine days when she was taken to the Yeoman Warder's House to await execution. Her husband was imprisoned close by in Beauchamp Tower and to this day you can see on the wall the letters J.A.N.E. – probably carved by the hand of her sad young husband.

From her window overlooking the Green, Jane saw her husband taken to his execution on Tower Hill. Later that same day the guards came for her, and with her ladies-in-waiting she walked proudly across Tower Green to the waiting executioner. A bandage was placed over her eyes – she groped for the block, saying, 'Where is it? What am I to do?' – and as she laid her head on the block she said, 'Lord into thy hands I commend my spirit.'

Although there are no prisoners in the Tower now, and it is no longer a place of execution, the famous ravens still flutter across Tower Green as they did on that morning when Jane walked to the scaffold. Today the ravens are the special responsibility of Yeoman Warden, John Wilmington.

Ravenmaster Wilmington looked as if he had stepped out of the pages of history himself – he could have been at the Tower in the days of Lady Jane Grey. A tall impressive north countryman with a great full beard, he wore the Tudor uniform of the Yeomen of the Guard – the Beefeaters, as they have been nicknamed for centuries.

Half a dozen ravens flapped and squawked around us, and on his wrist sat Hectora, a huge glossy black bird, who stared at me with fierce bright eyes.

'Can I touch her?' I asked.

'You can if you like,' said the Ravenmaster sardonically, 'but only if you want to lose a finger!'

I would have thought the ravens would be so used to the thousands of visitors who come to the Tower every year that they would be quite tame, but they are separated from the visitors by a fence – to protect the public from the ravens, maybe.

'What do you feed them on?' I asked.

'Mostly meat – we give them raw meat twice a day. They like beef best. I think *they're* the real Beefeaters, you know!'

The ravens come from remote half wild parts of Britain. They are gradually being exterminated, because people are rather frightened of such fierce birds, so enormous with their four foot wing span. But sometimes people find them as fledglings, and take them home. Then when they're too big to keep as pets, they offer them to the Tower.

The flight feathers on one wing are clipped so that they can't fly away. They live for about twenty-five years – probably much longer than they would live in the wilds.

'Isn't there a legend that says that if there are no more ravens in the Tower of London, there's going to be a terrible disaster to Britain? How did this start?'

'Well, ravens are scavengers by nature,' Ravenmaster Wilmington explained. 'In the old days, the White Tower had huge kitchens, and they threw out lumps of meat, and all the houses around threw out their scraps. There were so many ravens that the residents petitioned King Charles II to get rid of them, so he gave orders to have them destroyed. Then one of the old soothsayers pointed out that there was a legend here which goes back further than time itself, which said should all the ravens be killed a great disaster would befall England, and, worst of all, the White Tower itself would crumble into dust. Charles was rather superstitious, like the rest of them, so he gave orders that six ravens should be kept, and the remainder destroyed. So we have six ravens in the Tower to this day.'

In addition to the ravens the Tower used to have other animals, including lions, leopards, bears and even elephants – all gifts to the reigning monarch from far-off lands. Records in the Tower show that Henry I was presented with a white bear from Norway in 1252, and that some years later the King of France made him the gift of an elephant. The townspeople of London at the time took great delight in coming to the Tower to watch the elephant take its bath in the Thames.

By 1830 the Tower had two or three bears, a family of lions, one elephant, wolves, hyenas and a hundred rattlesnakes. To give them more space and better conditions they were moved along with some animals from Windsor Castle to Regent's Park. In this way, they formed the beginnings of London Zoo.

Blue Peter visits The Lord Mayor of London

Although these animals now live in Regent's Park Zoo, they are still very much a part of the heritage of the City, for many of them appear on heraldic crests and signs. Two gold fish fly on the roof of the fish market at

Billingsgate; a grasshopper sits perched above the Royal Exchange. The Ancient Orders of Guilds and Livery Companies, groups of merchants and tradesmen banded together to promote their interests, chose animals for their badges. The Merchant Taylors Company took two camels and a sheep, the Haberdashers two goats and a lion, while the Skinners' Coat of Arms was almost a zoo in itself – a leopard, a wolf and a lynx! These animals, carved in wood or stone, or gleaming in stained glass windows, still flourish in the City of London.

Guildhall

The traditional home of the Guilds and Livery Companies is Guildhall, the place where the City of London has had its government for more than one thousand years. Just think of the history this great hall has witnessed: the trial and sentence to death of Lady

Jane Grey, angry demonstrations for reform, countless brilliant receptions for Emperors, kings and statesmen that the City has wished to honour.

The banners of the Goldsmiths, the Drapers, the Mercers, and the twelve principal companies line the ancient walls, which luckily survived both the Great Fire of 1666 and the devastation of the Blitz of 1940. They have proudly looked down upon more than seven hundred Lord Mayors, including the legendary Richard Whittington – Dick Whittington himself.

He was Lord Mayor three times in the late fourteenth and early fifteenth century, and many legends have grown up about Dick and his cat. Certainly he was a very good and popular man, and over the years his fortune grew. But it's a bit doubtful whether he ever had a cat! French was widely spoken in the City in those days, and *le chat* certainly means cat in French – but *échat* means trade, which was very much a part of Dick Whittington's life. It's quite likely that story-

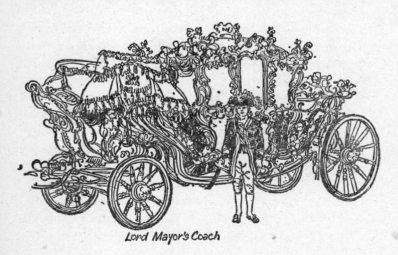

Lord Mayor's Coach

15

writers later confused *chat* with *échat* to produce the romantic legend we've all seen in pantomime.

It was five hundred years ago that Dick Whittington was made Mayor by the Guilds and Aldermen of the City, and on Michaelmas Day each year their successors still meet to choose the new Lord Mayor and then the preparations begin for the great day – the Lord Mayor's Show! The Show takes place on the second Saturday in November, and I was lucky enough to meet this year's Lord Mayor before he was presented to the City.

I was shown into a richly decorated room, and there waiting beside the fireplace was the Lord Mayor himself. He was wearing the scarlet-trimmed robes of an Alderman, and around his neck hung the great gold chain of office and the diamond-studded badge bearing the arms of the City of London. He was very charming, cheerful – and only the swiftest glance at his watch betrayed that he was a man about to keep a very important appointment!

I asked him how an ambitious young man can get to be Lord Mayor of London. Was there a sudden moment of triumph when he knew he was elected? He told me it wasn't really like that at all. 'Once you've become an Alderman of the city, if you live long enough and behave well enough, your turn will come. One day you'll be Lord Mayor. But of course you don't really know until you're elected – and that doesn't happen until September 29th, less than two months before the Show.'

'That doesn't leave you long to prepare,' I said. He smiled: 'Well, actually, I've been preparing for the last two years – just in case.'

A sleek black-and-white cat came purring in and rubbed against him. 'Fred,' said the Lord Mayor. 'Did you enjoy the kippers I left for you at breakfast?'

I looked at the Lord Mayor with his cat and remembered the chimes of Bow Bell:

> 'Turn again Whittington
> Thou worthy citizen
> Lord Mayor of London.'

The Bank of England and Petticoat Lane

As the Lord Mayor's Show winds its way slowly through the City streets, it passes close by most of the important buildings on which the wealth, power and reputation of London depend. And, secure in the heart of the City, the most important of them all must surely be the Bank of England.

This huge, fortress-like building houses the wealth of the City, and indeed of the whole nation, for behind its

Bank of England

walls lies untold wealth – thousands of millions of pounds' worth of gold, bank notes and securities held largely for the government.

Not surprisingly, *no one* is allowed inside; the strictest security is always observed. There was no question of the Blue Peter cameras being allowed to film within these walls.

Once, in 1786, the Bank of England did come under attack, during the Gordon Riots. After two unsuccessful attempts on it had been made by the rioters, a Bank Guard, or Picquet as it was called, was organized. It was mounted nightly by the Brigade of Guards, and at first it was most unpopular in the City. Every evening the Guard had to march two abreast along the crowded pavements of the Strand, Fleet Street and Cheapside, and 'jostled all who were in the way', the people complained.

Over the years, though, the sight of the guard marching from Wellington or Chelsea Barracks became a familiar and popular sight. For nearly two hundred years, every evening, the small detachment made its way along the City streets to guard the Bank's gold. In recent years marching through the City streets jammed with people and cars became more and more difficult, and so since 1959 the Picquet has travelled by army vehicle. Every evening, in full combat clothing, the guard still arrives to take up position for the defence of a fortune. The great doors shut on a wealth it is almost impossible to imagine – glittering rows of gold bars and bank notes worth millions of pounds.

But not all business in the City is done in millions . . .

Every Sunday morning there is a market in the City,

with goods of every kind piled high on stalls along the street, and bargains being offered by shouting, thrusting salesmen to the jostling crowds.

It is known as Petticoat Lane.

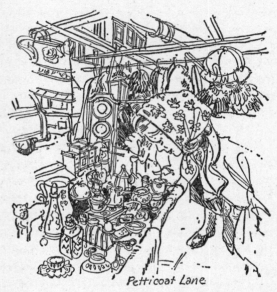

Petticoat Lane

There's an incredible range of things to buy in Petticoat Lane, and in some parts of the market groups of stalls all sell the same sort of wares – crockery, perhaps, or shirts, or records! Part of the process of buying there is to listen to the offers made – the 'spiel' they call it – and to bargain with the stall-holders for a lower price.

The first man I saw – or heard! – was shouting. 'Here you are! Here you are. Lovely blankets. Lovely blankets!' Every few minutes he would give a kind of strangled yell, so everyone turned round to look at him, and more people flocked to his stall. Behind him was a huge toppling pile of pale pink and blue blankets, wrapped in shiny polythene.

'What will you give me? Ten bob? Eight bob. Here's six bob. Five bob? Yer'll tell me when to stop, won't yer?' he bellowed. He kept to the old shillings and pence all the time – perhaps he thought it sounded cheaper.

'All right, then – half-a-crown for a pair of blankets!' But so many people wanted such a bargain he had to stop the rush. 'Where are you from, then?' he asked. 'I'll give them to the ones that have come furthest.'

One pair went to a lady from France, another to someone from Cumberland. Tourists and foreigners from all over the world pour into Petticoat Lane – it is one of the great sights of London on a Sunday morning. There are traffic jams for a mile around, in every direction, and we had to push through the crowds to take the cameras to the stalls to see what was going on.

By another stall, I saw a man piling boxes of sweets, tins of toffee, and packets of biscuits, into a carrier bag.

'Here you are then – all yours for just £1,' he announced. The carrier bag seemed bottomless – I was sure there must have been about £4 worth of goodies in each.

Suddenly, among the milling crowd, I caught sight of an impressive figure. It was a man in a dark suit covered all over with tiny pearly buttons: so many buttons I could hardly see the cloth of his suit. He held a collecting box, and was busy raising money for a charity. I went to talk to him and he said he was the Pearly King of the City of London. His dress was the traditional costume of many East Enders and City dwellers in former times on festive occasions. Once every district had its own Pearly King and Queen. He told me his suit had thirty-five thousand buttons, all sewn on by hand. He had done it himself, and it had taken him eighteen months. When he had finished, the suit weighed half a hundredweight.

But it is difficult to be a Pearly King nowadays. They don't make pearl buttons any more, they are nearly all some kind of plastic.

'Things,' said the Pearly King of the City of London sadly, 'ain't what they used to be!'

The Great Fire and The Great Cathedral

The hustle and bustle of Petticoat Lane is probably the nearest thing in London today to the atmosphere of the mid-seventeenth century when a fire broke out that dramatically changed the whole face of London.

At two o'clock in the morning on Sunday, September 2nd, 1666, a fire started in a baker's shop in Pudding Lane, in the heart of the City. The baker and his family climbed out on to the roof, and managed to escape, but sparks flew across Pudding Lane, which was just a narrow alley, into the courtyard of the Star Inn opposite, and set fire to piles of hay and straw kept for the horses. Sleeping neighbours awoke and started a chain of buckets, but the fire went on spreading. By eight o'clock leaping flames had attacked St Magnus' Church, and houses on London Bridge were ablaze.

The Lord Mayor of London, watching the proceedings on the spot, ordered buildings in the path of the fire to be demolished, as the fire could not shoot over empty spaces. No one obeyed him – no one wanted to destroy his own house; everyone was desperate to save his own family and his goods.

Householders piled furniture on to handcarts, blocking the narrow streets and hampering the firefighters. Boatmen charged extortionate fees to ferry people to safety over the river. Looting started. And still the fire spread, crackling, flaming, destroying everything in its path, choking and smothering everyone who got near it. There was nothing to fight it – no efficient engines, no long hoses, no reserves of water. Ashes and sparks were blown up river as far as Windsor; by nightfall the red glow in the sky could be seen as far away as Oxford.

The King himself, Charles II, came down on Monday and again on Tuesday. He flung a pocketful of guineas to the firefighters to encourage them, and then he got down from his horse and seized a bucket himself, getting his fine clothes soaked and filthy. He called in sailors from the Navy, and dockyard workers. The hesitation of the Lord Mayor, the obstructive tactics of the citizens, were ended – gunpowder was brought in, and whole blocks of buildings were blown up to make firebreaks. Appalled and fascinated, the panic-stricken refugees on the South Bank watched the devastation from across the river.

By Wednesday evening the fire was under control. By Thursday it was out. The horrified Londoners crept back to the wrecks of their houses. One hundred thousand were homeless; many were utterly ruined. There was no kind of fire insurance. Strangely, there had been little loss of life – only six people had been killed.

In the five days of the fire, thirteen thousand houses had been destroyed; the halls of forty-four of the City Livery Companies reduced to ashes; eighty-four churches were in ruins, and St Paul's Cathedral was a roofless, hollow shell.

What was to be done with the nation's Capital? How was the City to be rebuilt? It was a wonderful opportunity to make a new London, far more splendid than the old. There could be a complete new lay-out, and an improved street plan: gardens along the banks of the river; wide gracious squares with fountains playing, like an Italian city.

Christopher Wren prepared a plan for a new city – an ideal London for generations to come. The King approved, but Londoners were impatient to rebuild their houses and take up life again exactly as before. Merchants were eager to resume business as usual. No overall town plan was accepted and each property owner was free to rebuild on his own site. The chance was lost. Wren's master-plan for a new City was abandoned. Confusing, crowded, higgledy-piggledy London grew up once more.

But some of Wren's individual designs were accepted. Soon he was responsible for many new churches – rounded columns, delicate spires, steeples in endless variety began to point skywards again. Wren was responsible for rebuilding – re-creating – fifty-two of the City's lost churches.

To make sure the Fire was never forgotten, Londoners raised a great Monument, and this, too, Christopher Wren designed. It still stands, a great Doric column two hundred and two feet high – the exact distance from the Monument to the site of the baker's shop in Pudding Lane, where the Great Fire started. On top is a golden ball surrounded by flames. The column is hollow and from it, if you can climb the three hundred and eleven steps to the balcony at the top, you get one of the finest views there is of the City of London, with the river Thames, Tower Bridge and the many City churches Wren designed.

But Wren's masterpiece, beyond a shadow of a doubt, was his design for a new cathedral for London. His St Paul's is so much a part of London it is difficult to imagine what the City looked like without it. There has been a church on the site at the top of Ludgate Hill for thirteen hundred years, and before the Fire Old St Paul's was the largest church in England.

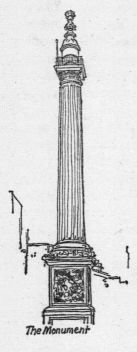
The Monument

When Christopher Wren was approached by the City Fathers, he is supposed to have replied at first that he was too busy building fifty-one other churches. Eventually he accepted the commission and then took thirty-five years to complete it. He presented the King and the City with plans for a far finer cathedral than the older one, revolutionary in design. It was to be the first church in the country surmounted by a vast dome.

The King liked the design, but no one else did. They distrusted the idea of a church without a steeple. Wren, who wanted to build a cathedral for London as splendid as St Peter's in Rome, persisted. But it was nearly ten years after the Great Fire before a plan was finally accepted. Wren included a very ornamental steeple in this design but still kept his dome, and he sent a letter with the plan, saying that as it would be difficult to build the church modifications might be necessary. The Royal Commissioners allowed Wren to start his new building, and to make 'variations rather ornamental than essential'. Wren fully intended that the first thing to go would be the steeple!

The site was cleared by knocking down the bits of Old St Paul's that still stood with great battering rams. Forty-seven thousand waggon loads of rubbish were dragged away, while Wren stood on a platform in the midst of the ruins directing his army of builders. As the fine new building began to rise, Wren took a little house across the Thames, and watched his cathedral grow from its windows.

It was impressive. It was five hundred and fifteen

St. Paul's

feet long and three hundred and sixty-five feet high. It towered above every other building in London, and the great dome began to dominate the City. It was a masterpiece of engineering. There was an inside dome on which a beautiful ceiling would be painted, then a brick cone built to support the Cross, and a false outer dome to complete the design. To inspect the work Wren would get in a basket, and be hauled by ropes up to the roof.

Finally the great day came when the building was completed. Wren was an old man now, but he lived to see his son place the last brick on the great dome and, instead of a steeple, his cathedral was crowned with a great golden Cross.

There is no statue of Wren in the Cathedral. He lies buried in the crypt, and the great church, with the High Altar under the magnificent cupola is the background of his memorial – an inscription in Latin, written by his son who was also called Christopher Wren: 'Si Monumentum Requiris, Circumspice' – 'If you seek his monument, look around you!'

A second chance

From the day Christopher Wren saw it finished, St Paul's stood dominating the skyline of London until one terrifying night – December 29th, 1940 – when London was struck by a hail of bombs. Britain was at war, and on that night German bombers dropped thousands of tons of high explosive on to the City beneath. People hurried to shelter, as all around them bombs were starting hundreds of fires. Water ran short and firemen fought desperately. Vast buildings were gutted in spite of their efforts, and the whole City seemed doomed. The flames grew nearer and nearer to the Cathedral.

St Paul's still stood, but surrounded by fire it seemed that it must be lost forever.

But when morning came, the great dome was un-damaged – St Paul's towered above a sea of rubble, a symbol of London's courage and defiance.

Some other churches that Wren had built were saved too – though the magnificent spire of St Dunstan's in the East, was the only part of that church that survived the blitz. In a way this would have made its designer particularly proud, for when St Dunstan's was built Wren was told by many doubting Thomases that the slender, beautiful spire would never endure. At that time many City steeples had been damaged or de-stroyed by a great storm.

'St Dunstan's will survive,' was Wren's confident reply. And for over three-hundred years it remained unimpaired; even the German bombs which destroyed the church left the spire untouched.

But many other spires and great buildings were not so lucky. Vast areas of the City were reduced to ruins. The City was full of bomb sites – shells of buildings, piles of rubble.

Again, London had a chance to rebuild. Once more there was an opportunity for a grand design – a plan that would incorporate the remaining undamaged his-toric buildings and bring new life and style to the City.

But because of the shortage of money and manpower in the post-war years there was no master plan and new buildings sprang up jostling one another in height and size.

Historic and beautiful spires are half-hidden and even the Tower of London will shortly be overlooked by a vast new hotel. It is now very difficult to find an uncluttered view of St Paul's. The dome still rises triumphantly above the towering new blocks, but instead of seeing the masterpiece as a whole it is now all too easy to catch a glimpse of only a part – fragments of a splendour which needs space and proportion to allow it to live.

And the building goes on. New office blocks have risen rapidly in recent years and because of an acute shortage of space the buildings grow taller and taller. Yet these are the buildings which are vital for the City's national banking and trading communities. The City's continued prosperity depends on these buildings and the people who work in them.

Each evening when the present-day citizens of London leave their offices, the streets are jammed with bustling crowds, all battling to leave the City as fast as possible. The army of workers is on the move again. The noise of impatient cars and buses reaches a crescendo until quite suddenly they've all gone. The traffic is light, the streets are deserted and the rush hour is over.

The City is quiet again. Before the Great Fire of London a quarter of a million people lived in and around these streets – now only four thousand people have their homes here.

The great buildings stand silent, guarding the wealth and fortunes of the proud City which in a few brief hours will ring again with the bustle and clamour of a new day.

AMSTERDAM

The Dutch have a saying, 'God made the world, but the Dutch made Holland.'

Certainly they're the only people who have built an airport on the site of a naval battle. The battle took place in 1573 between the Dutch and Spanish fleets, about fifteen feet above the runway where my plane touched down, when all the area that is now Holland's chief airport was covered by the waters of the North Sea.

Since then generations of Dutch engineers have drained and dyked the whole area. The sea-coast is now over twenty miles away, and there are 560 miles of underground piping to keep the runways dry. But as a reminder of all the ships that were wrecked here before the sea was driven back, Amsterdam's airport is called 'Schiphol' – the ships' grave.

The city on the water

Like its airport, Amsterdam is built on an unusual spot. In fact there seems no good reason for a large city to be here at all. The ground is marshy and difficult to build on; there are no natural resources in the area, and the city has never been the seat of government or the home of a king.

But this didn't stop the early Amsterdamers. They were determined to make their town beautiful, prosperous and powerful. They succeeded so well that today Amsterdam is recognized as the chief city of the Netherlands. As in other capitals, you can go sight-seeing by luxury coach, but it's more fun to take a boat. There are trips by water-boat every few minutes or you can hire a boatman to take you wherever you like – a sort of water-taxi.

My 'taximan' was Mr Kees de Rover. He was a splendid figure, very smart in dark blue uniform and a dark peaked cap. He had a grey fringe beard all round his jaw, and as he took his place on the boat I thought he looked like Mr Peggotty in *David Copperfield*. As we threaded our way through the network of canals, he pointed out the sights of the City in mixed English and

Canal scene

Dutch, which sounded real 'Double Dutch', but I was able to understand most of it!

He told me that Amsterdam began with a village built on the estuary of the River Amstel. To protect themselves from the fierce incoming tides of the Zuyder Zee the villagers built a dam. Amsteledam became Amsterdam – and with safe access to sea and river, the town flourished.

The dam was the making of the city. Goods had to be transferred from boats coming down the river into sea-going ships on the other side, and in this way Amsterdam came to specialize in water-borne trade.

There was no shortage of water, and as their town grew the Amsterdamers decided to take advantage of it. They dug canals right up to their front doors, laying them out just like roads, with side canals branching off the main ones. Altogether a hundred canals were cut. To cross them they erected a total of a thousand bridges. Many of these were designed to lift up, with large counter-balanced weights, so that the bigger boats could get through.

As a result you could reach almost every house by water.

The town council were so proud of their enormous canal network that at one time they decided to ban all horse-drawn traffic from the city centre. Visitors had to leave their carriages in one of the large parking squares on the outskirts, and then continue by boat. The rule didn't last long. Today the canal banks have become parking places – dangerous ones, too, for a driver only needs to forget his handbrake, and he could come back in the evening to find his car in ten feet of water. This happens to some unlucky motorist at least once a week.

I was glad to learn that the Amsterdam Fire Brigade have become very quick at pulling them out!

Although the canals were built to serve the houses on their banks, nowadays there are lots of people actually living on the water. Altogether Amsterdam has two thousand house-boats. Some of them are kept immaculately, with rooftop gardens and colourful paintwork. Others are old barges, provided by the town council as cheap overnight dormitories. They're used by the hundreds of young people and students who go to Amsterdam each summer.

One boat has been turned into a floating lost cats' home. In the harbour there's a floating hotel. And when one of Amsterdam's banks – the ones that handle money! – wanted its canal-side offices rebuilt it had the ingenious idea of moving on to a boat whilst the alterations were done.

The prettiest boats are undoubtedly the flower stalls on the Singel canal, floating on the water with their wares displayed for the passers-by on the canal bank to see them, and stop to buy them. Roses, gladioli, tulips, were piled up in great tiers of colour – their scent filled the air.

I noticed that all the canal-side houses had a few steps leading up to the front door, and I learnt that the ground floors have to be raised up a bit, so that the cellars are not flooded with water. The steps also give a clue to how rich the original owner of the house was. In the old days houses in Amsterdam were taxed according to how wide they were and whether they had a single or double flight of steps leading up to the front door.

Over the houses there are different symbols carved in

Dutch Gables

stone. It was the custom to indicate what sort of trade the owner followed by these symbols. You can also guess the age of each house according to the sort of gable it has, because fashions in gables kept changing. The earliest houses had a stepped gable, then someone invented the bell-shaped gable, and later still the neck-shaped gable was the most popular.

Most of these houses belonged to the rich sea-traders of Amsterdam, and they were used as office and ware-house too, so there's a loading winch built into all the gable ends. They were designed to hoist goods up to the store rooms in the attic. The Amsterdamers find them so handy for furniture removing that they still use them today! It's much easier to get a new piano delivered this way than by manhandling it up three flights of stairs.

I was keen to see what the houses looked like inside, and Kees told me that beside the Voorburgwal canal there was one open to the public. The Voorburgwal is the oldest canal in the city and the house looked very impressive from the outside, tall and narrow with five storeys in all. When I was inside, I could see why they needed those hoists! The staircases are much narrower and steeper than in Britain and even with nothing to carry I found it was quite difficult to keep my balance!

I'd come up into the main bedroom of the merchant's house. It must have been marvellous to wake up each morning and look out over a quiet canal, instead of a busy street. The only problem with these houses was the danger of damp, so the ground floor was often used only for an entrance hall and kitchen. The living room where the family spent most of its time was up on the first floor, out of harm's way. It was here that the family would hang its collection of oil paintings – all Dutch merchants loved to have paintings on the walls – sometimes scenes from the Bible, sometimes just family portraits.

The top two attic floors would normally be for other bedrooms, offices and storerooms. But the attic of the particular house I went into was rather out of the ordinary, as I discovered when I climbed the steep stairs.

There's nothing strange about the stairs, or about the attic door. But when you open it, you find yourself in a church! It's a real church too, and the surprising thing is that it seems so large. That's because it occupies the top floor of the merchant's house, *and* the attics of two smaller houses built behind it.

It's got everything a real church needs – including a full-sized organ, which is still in perfect condition, and is often used for concerts. The only thing that seems to be missing is the pulpit, but that's because the designers thought of a clever way of saving space. They built the pulpit into the side of the altar, and when it was required it just swung out. The mechanism is a bit stiff and heavy but it still works.

From the street outside no one would ever guess the existence of this surprising church.

Jan Hartman's house-the house of 'Our Lord in the Attic'

All three houses were built by a man called Jan Hartman in 1661. He lived in the front one himself, and rented off the other two. He and his family were Roman Catholics, and at that time there were deep religious divisions between Protestants and Catholics. The city of Amsterdam wanted to be as tolerant as possible, but even there Catholics were not allowed to worship openly. So when Jan designed his house he planned a secret church, where his family and friends could come safely for their services. They called it 'Our Lord in the Attic'.

35

Quite likely, some members of the Amsterdam town council *did* know about Jan's church, but as long as no members of the public found out they didn't mind, for they wanted everyone to be able to follow their own beliefs as much as possible, if only because religious ill-feeling was bad for trade.

Round about the same time, the council offered help to another religious group who were being persecuted, and let them build *their* church on the edge of the city. These were the Jews who had been driven out of Portugal. They were delighted to find such a warm welcome in the Dutch city, for here they were free to worship as they wished. Before long a thriving Jewish community had grown up.

Many of the Jews were merchants, and they added their skill and experience to the adventurous spirit of the Amsterdamers. In particular, there was a small group of traders in diamonds. They set up their workshops along the banks of the River Amstel, and were so successful that the diamond industry today is the most important in the city – and Amsterdam is recognized as the diamond capital of the world.

The gems are not mined in Holland – most of them come from Kimberley in South Africa – but it's in Amsterdam that they are cut. Only when a rough diamond has been shaped in a special way, with many different reflecting sides or facets, does it give off its beautiful sparkle. Ever since they came here the Jews have proved masters of this delicate skill.

The Jewish people were always made welcome by the Dutch, but they were not to escape persecution even in Amsterdam. Thirty years ago, during the Second World War, the troops of Nazi Germany conquered the Netherlands and occupied Amsterdam. They put into practice the ideas of their leader Adolf Hitler and began to attack the Jews. They confiscated their property, threw them into prison, and finally sent them in cattle trucks to concentration camps in Germany. There many of them were put to death in the gas chambers.

The Dutch were horrified by this cruelty, and many protested. Close by the Jewish Synagogue there stands today a statue of a Dutch workman – a memorial to the Amsterdam dockers who refused to work for the Germans because of what they were doing to the Jews. As a punishment they too were sent to the death camps.

The deportation of the Amsterdam Jews was all the more saddening because many of them had fled to Holland *from* Germany only a few years before, just to escape from the Nazis. Among them was a man called Otto Frank, who had brought his wife and two teenage daughters, Margot and Anne with him.

He managed to get a job in a small factory on one of the quieter canals and for a while he thought he and his family were safe. But when the Germans overran Holland, Mr Frank realized it was only time before they would all get their 'calling up papers' – the summons to the death camps in Germany. Their only chance was to hide, and fortunately Mr Frank knew of an excellent hiding place.

He told his wife and the girls to pack a few things. It was not safe to be seen in the streets with a suitcase, so they all wore as many clothes as possible. Anne packed her books and hair curlers into her school satchel to avoid suspicion. They made their way to the canal house where Mr Frank had his office and he told them to climb up the steep staircase to the top floor. The two girls had no idea where they were going or why. Mr Frank had decided it would be unfair to expect them to keep such a difficult and dangerous secret from their school friends.

Their father led them into what seemed to be a tiny boxroom. Then he took hold of a bookcase against the wall and swung it back to reveal a secret stairway. This led up into four attic rooms in the back part of the house that hardly anyone knew about. Just as Jan Hartman had built his secret church in an attic, Mr Frank had discovered a secret annexe where his family could hide until the war was over.

The rooms were small and cheerless and Mr Frank warned his family that there would be many problems. During the daytime his old colleagues were still working in the factory and offices below. So from 8.30 to 5.30 each weekday they would have to be very quiet, in

Anne Frank and the house she hid in

case any noise or movement betrayed them. They could cook on an old stove, for there was a laboratory lower down, and people outside would assume the smoke was coming from that. But the lavatory could only be used at night – when no one would hear the noise of it flushing.

Young Anne was horrified. She was a lively girl, who tended to make plenty of noise. Only a few weeks before it had been her thirteenth birthday. There'd been a party, and she and her friends had been to the cinema to see the wonder-dog Rin-Tin-Tin. She had received lots of presents – flowers, chocolates and books. Now, she realized, there would be no more parties, no cinema, no flowers or chocolate for a long time. All she had left were her books.

Strangely enough, her favourite book was one with blank pages. It was a birthday present from her father and mother who suggested she keep it as a diary. Anne was thrilled with the idea and began it straight away. She wrote down on the first page in 1942, 'Nobody will be interested in the unbosomings of a thirteen year-old schoolgirl, but I want to write.' And she did, keeping her diary faithfully for the next two years.

Mr Frank knew full well that the secret annexe was hardly big enough for Anne, Margot and his wife, but all the same they had decided to invite another Jewish family who were in danger of arrest to share it with them. They were called Mr and Mrs Van Daan, and they had one teenage son, Peter. He brought his pet cat, Nonschi, with him. Later, when things outside got even worse, and all Jews were being arrested, an old family friend, a dentist called Mr Dussel, also joined them.

In the factory below no one was surprised when Mr Frank didn't turn up for work. He had told everyone he was planning to flee with his family to Switzerland, and they assumed that was what he had done. They never dreamt he was in hiding just two floors above them. One of the few people who knew was his former secretary, a young Dutch girl, who still worked in the office below, hoping against hope that no one would hear any suspicious noises from upstairs. She had arranged with Mr Frank to come every evening after dark to bring food.

For Anne, her father and the others, the strain was terrible. Eight people in such a cramped space were always on top of each other and there was always the danger of discovery and the need to keep quiet. They were only human and often got bad tempered and irritable with each other.

In her diary, Anne tried to understand all this tension. She admitted she made the others angry because in the evenings, when the workmen and office staff had gone, she was often 'boisterous'. She wrote sadly, 'I am boisterous, so as not to be miserable all the time.' She knew she could never go out of doors – she could only gaze out at the world through the windows of the secret annexe, and envy the children who were still free to play happily in the street.

When I went to the secret annexe I saw Anne's bedroom – empty now, with the walls faded. She had to share this room with Mr Dussel the dentist, but she was determined that it should really be *her* room. She stuck magazine pictures on the walls to brighten them up a bit – and her pin-ups are still there, tattered after thirty years. I recognized a picture of Princess Margaret and

Princess Elizabeth who is now our Queen Elizabeth II. They were about the same age as Anne and her sister.

Anne drew up a prospectus for the annexe, pretending it was a sort of hotel, a 'temporary residence, open all the year round, with free board and lodging'. But often she would sit at the window all day long just thinking – and half hearing the old carillon of the nearby Westerkerk striking the quarter hours. At night-time even that was quiet. 'In the evenings,' Anne wrote in her diary, 'it is the silence that frightens me so.'

It was in the evenings, too, that they would all group round their tiny radio set to hear news of the war, broadcast from Britain by the BBC. They longed for the Germans to be defeated, so that the persecution of the Jews would stop, and they would be able to come out of hiding.

Then on June 6th, 1944 – D-day – the British and American armies landed in Normandy. For the first time it looked as if the Germans might be driven out of Holland. Anne found an old map among her school books and pinned it on the wall. She began to mark the line of the Allied advance. On July 21st, she wrote in her diary, 'Now I am getting really hopeful, now things are going well at last. Yes, really, they're going very well.'

But a fortnight later, Anne heard the sound she had always dreaded – the wailing siren of the Nazi police patrol! Perhaps one of the workmen downstairs had become suspicious, perhaps someone had seen a movement from outside and reported it. Whatever the reason, there was no escape for the eight hideaways in the secret annexe. Their two years of suffering and silence had been in vain.

Anne was escorted from the house with the others, hustled into a police van and taken to the station. There they were all put on the train for Germany.

Tragically, it was the very last convoy of Jews to leave Amsterdam before the Allied troops arrived to liberate the city. Only Mr Frank survived the concentration camp. Anne died in March 1945, only two months before peace was declared. But when her father went back to Amsterdam after the war his Dutch friends told him they had rescued some papers from the annexe, after the German troops had ransacked it.

Among these papers was Anne's diary.

Mr Frank read it with amazement. He knew only too well the horror and misery his young daughter had endured for the last two years of her life – yet her diary was full of faith and hope in the future. He decided to publish it, so that the whole world could read the brave words she had written.

'In spite of everything, I still believe that people are really good at heart. If I look up into the heavens, I think that it will all come right, that this cruelty will end, and that peace and tranquillity will return again.'

Organs, trams and a dinner with nineteen courses!

As I looked out of the window where Anne had stood so often, gazing wistfully at the children playing on the canal bank and longing to join them, I heard music.

There beside the canal was a great organ with a man turning a handle. It was decorated with crudely coloured wooden figures, and scrolls of gold paintwork.

Street Organ

Street organs have been popular in Holland since the end of the last century and you come upon them everywhere. They can play all sorts of music – old and new – because it's recorded on strips of folded card. The holes let air through to operate the pipes, the drums and the cymbals, rather like on a mechanical piano. The handle moves the card through the machine, and also pumps the bellows. The organs are a common sight in Amsterdam still, but today their sound is often drowned by the busy traffic.

Although the Amsterdam merchants planned their city for water-borne traffic, nowadays it needs a modern system of public transport. The answer is a streamlined fleet of trams, which thread their way through the traffic with deceptive ease. Even the system of buying a ticket has been streamlined – you get it in advance from a machine at the back by the tram stop. I must say I found the machine very complicated when I tried it out, but it does mean that there isn't a great crowd of people all trying to pay the driver, nor a conductor pushing along the car. On the tram you cancel your own ticket by inserting it in a small automatic printing machine by the door. Then you can sit back and enjoy the ride.

Tram-driving is quite a demanding occupation, and in Amsterdam it's done by both men and women. Our tram was driven by a woman. In theory the drivers have priority over all other traffic, and it's up to everyone else to keep out of the way. At sharp corners this can be quite unnerving. The driver rings the warning bell (which isn't very loud), switches on the flashing indicators (which aren't very big) and hopes for the best. It must be quite terrifying for foreign motorists.

Another disturbing thing about Amsterdam's trams takes place *inside* if you happen to sit over one of the points where the tram bends. Suddenly you find your feet moving round beneath you, which is a very odd feeling the first time it happens. But this system of double articulation means the trams can be extra long, and carry 250 people at a time.

The driver controls everything from the cab. There's a magnet brake to hold the tram at stops, and automatic door controls. She can announce the stops over a microphone, and has radio contact with the central depot in case of breakdowns, accidents or traffic jams. She also has to watch out for special traffic lights at the busier junctions – and, most important, has to change the points by remote control. This is done by sending an electric charge down through the rails to operate the points motor just before the tram reaches them.

The trams go everywhere in the city, criss-crossing the canal network – which calls for another bit of Dutch ingenuity. There is a modern equivalent of the old lifting bridge, designed to take all kinds of traffic, including trams. As the bridge comes back down into position, the lines slot together, and so do the overhead power cables.

All the trams terminate at the Amsterdam central station which is built on an artificial island on the edge of the port. This was and still is the heart of Amsterdam's prosperity. Before the Zuyder Zee was drained, ships sailed from the harbour straight out into the North Sea. Nowadays they use the twenty-mile long Nordsee Ship Canal.

This has never been the most obvious place for a major port. When Amsterdam first began to grow in the sixteenth century, London, Antwerp and Hamburg were all in much stronger geographical positions. The Dutch merchants were aware of this, and knew it would be difficult to capture much trade inside Europe. But this didn't discourage them – instead, they looked overseas.

On the old harbour front is a large warehouse build-

The Harbour

45

ing, which was the headquarters of the West Indische Compagnie – the Dutch West India Company. This company sent expeditions to the North East Coast of America. Here they bought an island called Manhattan from the Red Indians for just sixty guilders and built a trading post called New Amsterdam. It was the shrewdest bargain the shrewd Dutch merchants ever made. Thirty-eight years later, after one of the many wars between Holland and England. New Amsterdam was handed over to the British – and they re-named it New York!

A little further down the quay is another old warehouse. This belongs to the Dutch *East* India Company, founded in 1602. In Dutch their title is Vereenigde Oost-Indische Compagnie, and those initials can still be seen above the gateway to the warehouse, with the letter A on top, showing it was the company's Amsterdam depot.

The East India Company sent ships to develop the trade route round the Cape of Good Hope, where they set up a colony, to India, and China. They discovered New Zealand, naming it after one of the provinces of the Netherlands, and one sea-captain, Tasman, gave his name to Tasmania. But their most important find was the islands of Indonesia, which the company called the Dutch East Indies. They soon became famous throughout Europe for their rare spices, rich materials and exotic foods.

Bali is one of the most beautiful islands of Indonesia – and it's also the name of one of the best restaurants in Amsterdam, where you can try out real Indonesian cooking. The great speciality in these restaurants is called a *rijstafel*, which means rice-table. It's based on

46

rice, like Indian and Chinese food, and there's quite a bit of curry, but the difference is that instead of just two or three side dishes of meat, vegetables and fruit, you get served with nineteen!

When I went to the Bali, my waiter was a small Oriental figure all in white, apart from a splendid multi-coloured turban that reminded me of a Paisley scarf. He carried a dazzling white napkin over his shoulder and flicked and flourished it with great effect.

As the trays arrived, loaded with dishes full of spicy, exotic food, everything looked and smelt marvellous, but I had no idea what it all was. My waiter pointed to the dishes and in a soft quiet voice explained them all to me. 'Nasi-rice,' he said. 'Pisang goreng, fried bananas. Katjang-peanuts' – and he went on and on, showing me sateh, meat on sticks such as I had eaten in Singapore, and chicken, and prawns, and pork, and endless dishes of vegetables.

I set to work to sample them all – and I thought every one delicious.

Street scene with bicycles

After a meal like that I was badly in need of some exercise, so I thought I'd try out the most popular way of getting about in Holland – the bicycle.

As the country is almost completely flat, it's a cyclist's paradise. In Amsterdam there are over 400,000 bikes, one for every two members of the population, and the city has lots of special cycle tracks. Like the trams, the bikes have their own traffic lights at the busiest cross-roads, and at the bike rush-hour, which is when all the children come out of school, they're very necessary.

On my bike, I rode to see something else the Amsterdam traders found on their voyages round the world. This discovery came from the Near East, in Turkey, and was the most profitable they ever made. You couldn't eat it, wear it, or make anything with it – but the Dutch realized that people would always want to buy something as beautiful as the tulip!

The bulb fields begin almost on the outskirts of Amsterdam and the most famous are about fifteen miles west of the City. Nowadays all kinds of flowers are grown – daffodils, hyacinths, irises – but a good half of the total are still tulips.

As I was riding along looking at the flower fields I saw a strange thing. Workers in one of the fields were tearing the heads off a beautiful crop of purple hyacinths and throwing them carelessly into a basket. I knew that if flowers are to keep well they must be correctly cut so I rode down into the field to find out what was going on.

The man in charge was the owner, Mr Dirk Lefeber. He told me the fields were producing *bulbs* to be sold all over the world. When flowers appeared, they were cut off at once, so that the strength of the plant stayed in the bulb, and more secondary bulbs developed along the original parent bulb. As these matured they were marketed all over the world. Many of them would find their way to gardening shops in Britain.

A bulb field

But Mr Lefeber doesn't just mass-produce existing bulbs. He spends much of his time trying to develop new strains of tulip, and in his greenhouse on the edge of the field he showed me some of them. The greenhouse was full of tulips I had never seen before, in a complete rainbow of colours, shading from vivid reds and orange to delicate pastels.

Mr Lefeber proudly showed me a lovely bloom. 'Lily-flowering,' he murmured. 'Quite, quite new. It just opened this morning, you know, it's still getting bigger.' The flower would last for about a week or ten days in full bloom, but it had taken many years to reach that state of perfection.

Different kinds of established tulips are crossed to produce a new variety. I asked how it was done.

'I can show you,' cried the bulb grower. 'From this tulip that is a very strong stem, and a strong flower, we put the pollen out of it on to this one – a bigger flower, but not so strong in the petals. So – we just put the pollen on. Maybe this one will be one of our best crossings!'

As simple as that – but it takes a very long time. It can be five or six years before a single plant in a new variety flowers. Then it takes another ten years to grow about a thousand, and yet another ten years to build up a stock of a million bulbs. Only then can it be called a trade variety, and be marketed. So it is twenty-five years after Mr Lefeber discovers a new variety of tulip that you or I can buy it in our local shop.

But there are plenty to be going on with. 'How many varieties of tulip are there already in the world?' I asked.

'Oh, so many thousands, thousands. More than a hundred thousand,' the tulip expert told me.

Mr Lefeber explained that if I wanted to get some idea of the size and variety of the Dutch flower industry I should visit the Amstel Park, where the Floriade Exhibition was being held.

The Floriade is an enormous international garden show, organized by the Dutch Horticultural Council and the City of Amsterdam, but it isn't just a park full of flowers and shrubs. When the flower-growers chose the site on the outskirts of the city they decided to make their Exhibition a place where everyone could have a good time, so as well as thousands of flowers I found lots of other attractions.

There was a display of animals from Amsterdam Zoo, watched by a great crowd. In another section I saw a demonstration of land drainage. There was an Archimedes screw, which can lift water up from one level to the next. Next to it there's a tall pole, showing the level of sea-water that would rush in and cover Amsterdam, if it weren't for the drains and dykes. The highest mark shows the sea level in 1953, when many dykes burst, and a large part of Holland was flooded.

There's plenty of water in the Floriade and one way of getting around to see the flowers was by water-bike. But there's also a miniature railway in the park, and as I thought I'd done enough pedalling for one day, I took a trip on that.

The Dutch have been growing flowers now for so long there's not much they can't do with them. For instance, by using a special heat treatment they can make bulbs flower at any time of the year. So it doesn't matter when you go to the Floriade, there are always hundreds of different flowers in bloom – like never ending Spring!

Windmill

Next to the Floriade is one of the few remaining windmills in Amsterdam.

Before the invention of steam power, the windmill was the principal source of energy in Holland, as there were no fast-running streams to turn water wheels. At one time the city had over 150 mills – grinding corn, sawing wood, processing oil, tobacco and cocoa. Many of them were also needed to pump up water from the low-lying fields into the dykes, using an Archimedes screw like the one in the Exhibition.

The most famous man that has ever lived in Amsterdam was a miller's son, though he was not a miller himself. He was a painter – perhaps the greatest painter the world has ever known, and his name was Rembrandt.

The Dutch are proud of Rembrandt in exactly the same way the British are proud of Shakespeare, because he represents for them the best their country has ever produced. As a young man he used to go for walks along the River Amstel by the mill, and make sketches of everything he saw. But the Dutch were not then really interested in buying landscapes so it was as a portrait painter that Rembrandt first made his name among the merchants of Amsterdam.

The wealthy Amsterdamers wanted paintings of themselves and their wives to hang in their canal-side homes. It was rather like having a wedding photo taken today. That kind of work paid very well. Rembrandt was soon taking on assistants to help him, and getting commissions from the leading art dealers. In 1634 he married the daughter of one of them, Saskia van Uylenburgh, and soon after they moved into a magnificent large house, where he established his studio.

He still had money to spare for his own private hobby, collecting. Then as now, Amsterdam was full of shops selling antiques and curios. Rembrandt loved to visit them all, on the look-out for anything unusual – a fine velvet cloak, a piece of medieval armour, or an old oil painting. Everything he liked he bought and took home.

His new house began to look like an antique shop and art gallery itself as his collection became one of the largest in Amsterdam. But he didn't just buy things to admire them; he also wanted to use them in his paintings. He painted his father, the miller, dressed up as an old warrior in a costume he had found in a junk shop. He painted Saskia, his wife, dressed up as Flora, the goddess of flowers, with a crown and a bouquet. Even in those days the Dutch were delighted by beautiful flowers.

Saskia inspired many of Rembrandt's great paintings and sketches, but, sadly, she was not physically strong. After only eight years of marriage she died, leaving Rembrandt with a seven-month old baby, a boy called Titus. For a time Rembrandt found it impossible to paint. He had lost both a loving wife, and his favourite model.

But fortunately he was working at this time on a portrait far larger than he had ever done before. The commission had come from some of the most influential citizens of Amsterdam – and Rembrandt knew it was the chance he had always wanted, to try out his ideas on a really big scale.

He advertised for a housekeeper to help look after

Titus and determined to finish the painting. Today it is the most precious work of art in all Amsterdam, and has pride of place in the Dutch National Gallery – the Rijksmuseum. The Museum has over five thousand paintings by the world's greatest artists, and over a million other works of art, but none is as famous or as valuable as Rembrandt's 'Nachtwacht' – 'The Night Watch'.

It's a strange picture – nothing like the usual group portrait of the day. It shows the Militia Company of Captain Frans Banning Cocq turning out for a royal visit by the French Queen Marie de Medici. The Militia were not professional soldiers, but wealthy citizens who had volunteered to serve in an emergency, a bit like the Home Guard in 'Dad's Army'. From the start Rembrandt wasn't satisfied with just painting them. He wanted the portrait to be full of action, so he added a crowd of extras, like a little girl running round with a chicken tied to her belt! He made other changes. Although it's called 'The Night Watch', it's not really

The Rijksmuseum

night-time. There are patches of sunlight. Then the men are not wearing uniform, but an assortment of colourful hats, doublets and bits of armour of the kind Rembrandt loved to collect.

All in all Rembrandt did everything in his power to make a straightforward portrait into an exciting work of art, and most critics agree that he succeeded. It is a unique painting, full of movement, a masterpiece of light and shade, and a million people come from all over the world to see it every year.

They don't see it quite as Rembrandt intended, because it used to be slightly bigger. In the museum there is a copy of the painting which was made by one of Rembrandt's pupils, and this is wider than the actual picture. There are two strips at each side which aren't there on the full-size version.

The explanation for this is rather sad. Once, long before the 'Night Watch' came to the safety of the Rijksmuseum, it was hung in the Town Hall. It was slightly too large for the wall, so two strips were cut off and thrown away. No one can possibly say how much the 'Night Watch' is worth today, but even those bits would certainly have been worth a small fortune.

All Rembrandts are extremely valuable, and the Rijksmuseum is fortunate to have such a large collection. One of the most splendid is called 'The Holy Family at Night'. It shows Mary and the Baby Jesus in a simple peasant room, lit by a fire and a single candle. You can't see the flame of the candle, but you can see the remarkable glow that Rembrandt has created with his yellow paint. In this technique he probably outclasses any other artist before or since. It is a work of genius.

But you can't run a business on genius alone. The number of commissions coming to Rembrandt's studio had begun to fall. The Dutch had just fought a costly war against Oliver Cromwell's English Republic and people had less money to spend on portraits. Rembrandt was getting old and found it difficult to adjust to this. He still visited the antique shops every week, and could not stop himself buying the things he liked – even if it meant borrowing money. He also had instalments to pay on the house and before long he was badly in debt.

Rembrant - Self portrait

In the end the house and all its contents had to be sold. A Bill of Sale was drawn up, listing all his wonderful collection. It looked as if Rembrandt's career was at an end. But there were two people who still loved him very much and they were determined he should not give up painting.

The first was the woman he had employed as house-keeper after Saskia's death. Her name was Hendrickje, and she was a kind cheerful person. The other was Titus, now a boy of seventeen. Between them they decided to take his father in hand. They declared they would be partners in a picture-dealing business, with Rembrandt as their employee. They would look after the bills and the money, whilst Rembrandt went on painting with nothing to worry him.

In Amsterdam, there is a Madame Tussaud's Wax-work Museum, with a special display of Rembrandt. One section shows the painter, as he was at this time of his life, working on one of his last and most famous portraits – a portrait of himself. Throughout his life when there was no one else to paint, he had always used himself as a model. As a young man, he tried to show how his character was revealed by the glance of his eye or the tilt of his head. He painted himself richly dressed in prosperous times – and finally, in old age, he still studied how time had changed the face he knew best.

He died in 1669 in a quiet street in the shadow of the Westerkerk. Thanks to Hendrickje and Titus he had kept on painting to the end. But he knew how near to tragedy his own foolish extravagance had brought him, and he never forgave himself.

Looking back, many people now see the time of Rembrandt as Amsterdam's Golden Age. It was certainly an age of great achievement – in trade, in art, and in architecture. It was then that the great carillons of Amsterdam were built. They were the work of two brothers Francis and Pieter Hemony, who were born in Paris – but who fled to Holland when the French King

57

began attacking the Protestants. In Holland they started a bell foundry that became the most famous in Europe.

A carillon is a peal of bells fixed high up in a church steeple. They do not ring patterns of notes, or 'changes' like English bells, but play actual tunes, and these can be heard echoing high over the roofs of the canal-side houses throughout the city.

A carillon is played from a manual rather like an organ, but the keys are much bigger and have to be thumped. Recitals are still given every week, and Mr Ligt, one of Amsterdam's most popular carillon players, allowed me to watch him.

It must be very strange to give a concert 120 feet above ground, with no visible audience. In fact, it's only by keeping the trap door above his head open that Mr Ligt can hear clearly what he's playing.

Altogether there are five carillons built by the Hemony brothers in the city, all carefully preserved. They're a reminder, like the canals and the old merchants' houses, that Amsterdam was once the richest city in the world – bigger, in 1650, than Rome, Vienna or London – and just as famous for its art as for its trade.

Today Amsterdam is one of the smallest European capitals but it's still one of the most impressive. Modern Amsterdamers have a real pride in the great achievements of the past, yet they're every bit as forward-looking and enterprising as their ancestors in the city's Golden Age.

EDINBURGH

Edinburgh is one of the most famous and beautiful cities of Europe, and the capital of Scotland. Although I had been to Edinburgh before, I felt almost as much a stranger there, because I am English, as I had in any capital city I visited on any of the Blue Peter Special Assignments.

Even though England and Scotland have been united for 370 years, Edinburgh is very much the capital of another land, with its own law, its own Church, its own language, music, food and drink.

Edinburgh Castle

Rising from the midst of Edinburgh's busy traffic is the Castle Rock – dark, grey forbidding rock of some extinct volcano, it soars up 270 feet from the shops and monuments of bustling Princes Street. At the foot of the rock there are trim green gardens. Perched on the summit is Edinburgh Castle, a fortress and a refuge for more than twelve centuries. King Malcolm, successor to Macbeth, lived here, with his wife, beautiful, saintly

The Castle

Margaret. The chapel she built in 1076 is still here, the oldest building in Edinburgh still in use.

The castle is the heart of Edinburgh and in the heart of the castle are Scotland's own Crown Jewels, which are the oldest in Europe. They are kept in a room known as the King's Lodging, overlooking the old palace yard. The Crown, the Sceptre and the Sword of State make up the Honours of Scotland, as they are properly called.

The Crown is made of Scottish gold, resplendent with ninety-four pearls, ten diamonds and thirty-three other sparkling stones. It was remodelled in 1540 by King James IV of Scotland, grandfather of Mary Queen of Scots. Even the velvet cushion on which it rests is three hundred years old. Close beside it gleams a ring of diamond and ruby. This, tradition says, is the Coronation Ring of King Charles I, Queen Mary's tragic grandson, executed, like her, in England.

The Honours of Scotland have not always been in

the castle. At various times in Scotland's stormy history, they were taken away for sake-keeping. Once, to keep them out of Cromwell's hands, they were buried under the floor of a church, and there they stayed for nine years.

Always at the sittings of the Scottish Parliament, the Crown Jewels appeared in all their glory, but in 1707 the Scottish Parliament was merged with the English Parliament at Westminster, and the Scots were afraid that the Honours of Scotland might be carried away to England. So they were fastened up in a strong oak chest, with massive locks, and then they were forgotten for 111 years. In 1818, Walter Scott, Scotland's greatest novelist, sought Royal permission to open the treasure chest. There lay the Honours of Scotland – tarnished, but safe and undamaged.

The chest still stands in the Crown Chambers of Edinburgh Castle. The Honours of Scotland shine and sparkle on their velvet cushions. But they are still sometimes displayed in ceremonial triumph. In 1953, Coronation Year, the Honours of Scotland were carried in procession from the Palace of Holyroodhouse to St Giles Cathedral, and there offered to Her Majesty Queen Elizabeth II.

In the room next to the Crown Room, James, son of Mary Queen of Scots, was born. Mary reigned in Scotland for only seven stormy years. Then she fled from her war-torn kingdom, hoping to find safety with her cousin Elizabeth, Queen of England. Instead, she found imprisonment, and death on the scaffold nineteen years later.

Elizabeth had no children, and her only heir was the son of her cousin Mary, whom she had executed. So

Mary's son, James VI of Scotland became King James I of England in 1603; the first king of the two united Kingdoms.

But Scotland refused to be absorbed into England, and to this day, Scotland remains stubbornly Scotland.

Edinburgh Castle bristles with guns. The best known has a name – it is called Mons Meg, and tradition has it that it was forged within the Castle by Robert Borthwick, master gunner to James IV. When Mons Meg was in action in the fifteenth century, she could hurl a stone cannon ball 3,000 yards.

But the castle also has modern guns, and one of them is fired every day. It's called the 'time-gun', and is known locally as the 'one o'clock gun'. On the ramparts of the castle overlooking the city I talked to Mr Deans, a man with a magnificent moustache, whose job it is to fire the famous one o'clock gun.

Every day (apart from Sundays and Bank Holidays) since 1861 the one o'clock gun has boomed out over the city. The original idea was a signal to the ships in the Firth of Forth so that the Captains could set their chronometers to the exact time. The prevailing east wind carries the sound of the gun conveniently across the new town and down the river. But in case the wind is in the west a ball is dropped in a tower on a neighbouring hill at precisely the same moment. However, when I was there in August the gun went off at British Summer Time and the ball dropped down at Greenwich Mean Time. I don't know what the Captains on the Forth made of this, but it certainly confused me!

Today, of course, all the ships are fitted with radios, so the one o'clock gun isn't relied on as it used to be. But the citizens of Edinburgh all use it as a time check, and when the gun roars out you can see them glance down at their watches, as I do when I hear the pips on the radio.

Edwin of Northumberland built the first castle on the site over a thousand years ago, and gave the town his name: EDWINBOROUGH. Ever since then a castle has stood, guarding the town and commanding the river Forth which runs into the North Sea.

Today on the shores of this great river stands Europe's largest and newest power station built on land reclaimed from the sea.

At Queensferry – a few miles upstream from the city – is the Old Forth Bridge. In its time it was one of the engineering wonders of the world. Now beside it stands a new marvel – the new road bridge – the longest single span suspension bridge in the world.

On a clear day you can see right across the river to the ancient Kingdom of Fife, where all the early Scottish kings lived. It was on these shores at Leith, which is Edinburgh's harbour, that Mary Queen of Scots landed when she was nineteen, returning from France to claim her kingdom.

It was a great occasion. Mons Meg fired a salute for

The Forth Bridge

the home-coming of the young girl who has had a place in every Scotsman's heart from that day onwards.

Two famous walks

Because Scotland could never rely on the road south through England, she has always been linked to Europe by sea, and it was from distant seas that Norwegian whalers brought to Edinburgh something no one in Europe had seen before. It was a bird, a bird that could not fly, and that swam in the Antarctic Ocean. A penguin.

In 1914 six penguins were brought to Edinburgh Zoo, and the first ever penguin colony in captivity was established. For two years they flourished, and then in 1916 Edinburgh Zoo was able to announce the arrival of the first penguin chicks hatched out in captivity.

The keeper in charge of the penguins today is Mr Kennedy, who told me that there are now 134 birds in the colony, which includes eighty-nine Gentu, three King Penguin, and ten Rock Hoppers. They breed

Penguins at Edinburgh Zoo

regularly every year, nesting on specially made concrete rings filled with pebbles. The nests didn't look all that comfortable to me, but Mr Kennedy said that the penguins were very happy sitting on their concrete and pebbles, just like the rocks and stones they would use in Antarctica!

But Edinburgh Zoo has another unique penguin story – one that started by accident. Many years ago, a keeper left the gate open by mistake and the penguins, being curious birds, hopped out of their enclosure to see what the rest of the world looked like. They strolled around the Zoo quite unconcerned among the delighted visitors, and then quietly filed back home for tea!

That established a tradition.

Every day since then the gate has been opened at 3.30 PM and the penguins go out for their famous 'walk'.

'There's no compulsion about it,' said Keeper Kennedy. 'Every walker is a volunteer.'

Another famous walk (although not for Penguins!) in Edinburgh is the green stretch known as the Meadows, where everyone seems to play Scotland's national game – Golf.

The origins of golf seem lost in time, but James IV and James V, the grandfather and father of Mary Queen of Scots, both played, and Mary herself was a keen golfer who practised frequently. Her son James VI played on the meadows in Edinburgh, and when he went south as King of England he took golf with him. The new fashion spread and today Scotland's Royal and Ancient Game is played throughout the world.

In Edinburgh, the Honourable Company of Edinburgh Golfers, founded in 1744, is one of the oldest golf clubs in the world – and in Scotland golf was never a game for the exclusive few, but was always played by rich and poor, old and young. Whilst in the rest of the world there are long waiting-lists for the privilege of paying enormous subscriptions to join an exclusive golf club, back in Edinburgh's Meadows you can get a round of golf anytime you like for precisely nothing.

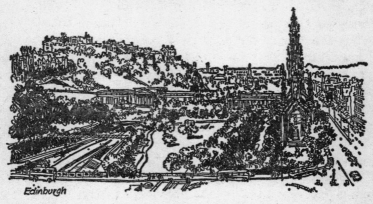

Edinburgh

I was there during the school holidays, and there were about twenty children playing whose ages ranged from six to about thirteen. As a non-golfer, I've always thought of the game as smart, middle-aged and respectable, but here it was as gay and abandoned and noisy as any Saturday morning football match. Indeed, the same children play football on the Meadows during the winter.

'It's football in the winter and golf in the summer, d'ye see?' one six-year-old explained. Golf clubs, the kind you play with, are expensive, so I asked how they managed to afford them.

'We get them one at a time for birthdays and that,

and then we borrow off each other.' It seemed odd to see that glazed look of dedication that marks the concentrated golfer on faces so young. I asked one of them if he wanted to be a professional golfer when he grew up. He looked at me and laughed as a gust of chilly east wind blew his hair across his face.

'No, of course not,' he said. 'I want to be a pearl diver!'

A medical scandal

Originally, the Meadows lay just outside the old city wall, and in those days they were the burial ground for plague victims.

Just beyond lies the Medical School.

Edinburgh has one of the earliest and most famous schools of medicine in the world. Its reputation today is still enormous, but back in 1828 a scandal took place that shook Edinburgh and rocked the medical world. It began with Doctor Robert Knox, who had become one of the leading lecturers in anatomy in Edinburgh. Students flocked to his classes in the College of Surgeons' lecture rooms, as many as 500 at a time.

For his lectures, Dr Knox needed human bodies to dissect, and of course they were very hard to obtain. It was not long before a hideous trade developed – grave-robbing!

Several of the churches in Edinburgh built watch-towers and mort-safes where a guard would be set at night, to prevent men from coming to the graveyard after a funeral, opening the grave and stealing then selling the body. The thieves were called the bodysnatchers, the resurrectionists or the 'sack 'em up men'.

Society and the law shut its eyes to the problem.

At that time an Irishman, William Hare, kept a lodging house in Tanner's Close. One day one of his lodgers, an old soldier, died, owing him money. Hare talked to another lodger, called Burke, and told him he was going to take the old man's body to the 'doctors'. They would give money for it and that would pay off the debt.

That night Burke and Hare delivered the body in a sack and they were paid £7.10 in gold. It was an eye-opener to Burke. He saw a royal road to riches: easier than work, safer than grave-robbing. The demand was there; he would supply it.

The pair turned to murder. For a nightmare year Burke and Hare ran their hideous trade. People were lured to the lodging house – people who would not be missed, and about whom no questions would be asked. And then at night, on a handcart, the bodies would be trundled across Edinburgh to the 'doctors'. Fear and suspicion grew to whispers: whispers grew to rhymes.

Up the close and down the stair.
But and ben with Burke and Hare –
Burke's the butcher, Hare's the thief –
Knox the boy that buys the beef.

Then, one gloomy day in November, it all happened once too often. Police arrived and searched Hare's lodging house. The bodies in the dissecting room were examined. Burke and Hare were arrested, and flung into prison. But even now, there was not enough evidence against them. So Hare was persuaded to turn

King's Evidence – that is, he was promised that if he told everything he knew about Burke, he himself would be allowed to go free.

The trial of William Burke the murderer took place in the Court House in Parliament Close, on December 24th, 1828.

He was said to have committed sixteen murders. The chief witness against him was his ally and accomplice, William Hare. On the next day – Christmas Day – Burke was condemned to death, and his body ordered to be dissected. He was hanged a month later, before an enormous crowd, and his body given to the 'doctors'. I saw his skeleton, which is still preserved in the Surgeons' Museum, in Edinburgh.

Hare fled to London, and is supposed to have died in want. And so the brief but ghastly episode was over.

Science and the law were both satisfied – and the reputation and skill of the Edinburgh doctors recovered and eventually grew higher than ever.

The old town and the new town

On a sunny day, I climbed the Outlook Tower, high up the Royal Mile, close by the Castle. At the top of a staircase I was shown into a small, dark room, with about a dozen other visitors. Dimly I could see in the centre what looked like a large, round, white table, but as my eyes grew used to the gloom, I saw the surface was covered by moving pictures.

Then I could see trees, and buildings I recognized, and cars, and I realized I was looking at a picture of Princes Street, far below the Outlook Tower.

This was Edinburgh's famous Camera Obscura.

Mirrors are fixed outside the tower reflecting the scene outside. By lenses the image is thrown on to the curved surface of the 'table'. The picture is coloured, moving, exactly as it is at that very moment, but strangely shadowy and silent. The picture changes direction, so you are shown a moving panorama of all the surroundings of the Tower, on every side.

All Edinburgh is thrown on to this shadowy silent screen, in the mysterious twilight of the Dark Room – which is what Camera Obscura means.

To see Edinburgh properly you have to get up high, so that you can look down on the castle, and the Royal Mile, a narrow hog's back of rock a mile long, running between the castle at the top and Holyrood Palace at the bottom.

It was at Holyrood, the royal residence of the Stewart Kings and Queens of Scotland, that much of Scotland's violent history was made.

Along the narrow mile of rock, the Old Town of Edinburgh grew up. After the terrible Battle of Flodden, when so many brave Scotsmen were killed by the

Holyrood Palace

victorious English, there was an urgent cry to strengthen the defences even further and a city wall, the Flodden Wall, was built in haste. Protected by the Flodden Wall, Edinburgh was in a marvellous defensive position, but inside the wall space was scarce. The only way to grow was up; and up they went, like New York 400 years later! The old houses in Edinburgh were the first sky-scrapers in Europe, for they were built up and up, six, seven, eight storeys high, with as many as ten families living on top of each other, and sharing a common stair.

The Old Town

The Scottish peers had their grand town houses in the Royal Mile, but when Scotland and England became one, the Scottish Peers left Edinburgh for London, and much of Edinburgh's prosperity went with them. It became a mean, over-crowded city, choked with houses. The Royal Mile became a slum. One day, the side wall of a building six storeys high collapsed. Not many people were killed, but everyone had had enough. The citizens of Edinburgh decided to build a New Town.

By an Act of Parliament they were permitted to extend the boundaries of the city. They begged and borrowed money and suddenly this poor, mean, little-known capital blossomed. They removed the markets and the shambles: they turned the Castle Loch into gardens. The new Edinburgh became known as the Athens of the North, and remains one of the most beautiful cities in Europe.

Scott's Monument

The citizens of Edinburgh built many statues to the heroes of the city and to the men who had created the New Town and lived and worked there. Some are ridiculous, some sublime, some simple and some astonishing. A statue of King Robert the Bruce, who gave Edinburgh the Port of Leith by Charter in 1369 stands on guard at the castle. Sir Walter Scott, the novelist who made the world aware of Scotland's romantic history, presides in Princes Street, seated under a towering Gothic spire, with his deerhound Maida beside him. There are statues to

David Livingstone, the Scot who opened up Africa, to Sir James Simpson, who discovered chloroform, and to Ensign Ewart, the soldier who captured singlehanded a Napoleonic eagle in battle.

Perhaps the most remarkable statue of all is to Greyfriars Bobby a little Skye terrier who could not forget his master.

Greyfriars Bobby

Bobby was a real dog, and he lived on a farm in the hills just south of Edinburgh. He belonged to the farmer, but he spent all his time out on the hills with the farm's shepherd, Old Jock.

Every Wednesday Old Jock would come into Edinburgh to the weekly sheep market. When the one o'clock gun sounded up in the castle, the shepherd and his dog would go to Greyfriars Dining Rooms, kept by a Mr Traill. Jock would buy a meal, and Mr Traill always found something for Bobby too.

But the shepherd at last grew too old for work and was paid off by the farmer, who brought him and Bobby into Edinburgh. This time, Jock didn't go back to the farm, but stayed in town when Bobby, with his official master, left.

When Bobby discovered on the homeward journey that Jock wasn't in the cart too, he was terribly worried. What could have gone wrong? Determined to find out, he slipped out of the cart and went trotting back along the road to Edinburgh. He searched for Jock in all the places he knew, and at last he found him – sleeping in a close near the Grassmarket. Bobby was overjoyed, but old Jock was very ill. They went to Greyfriars Dining Rooms, and Mr Traill, very concerned, went off to fetch a doctor – but old Jock was suspicious of doctors and when Mr Traill came back, Jock and Bobby had vanished.

Days later, Jock was found in an attic room: dead. His Bible with his name in it lay beside him, and Bobby was crouched down by his bed, keeping guard over his body. Old Jock was buried in Greyfriars Churchyard, and a headstone stands there today, marking his grave.

Three days after his funeral, as the one o'clock gun from the castle died away, a worn, distressed little dog hurried into Traill's Dining Rooms. Mr Traill tried to call him, and put down food. Bobby snatched the food, and rushed away. This went on for several days. At last Mr Traill followed the dog, to see where he went and Bobby led him to Old Jock's grave! Bobby was living in the churchyard, going each night to lie on the grave. During the daytime he was chased off by the caretaker.

Touched by the sight of the lonely little dog, Mr Traill took him all the way back to the farm – but it was no use. In a couple of days Bobby was back again, keeping his watch on the grave of his dead master. So he was accepted. James Brown, the caretaker, made friends with him. Mr Traill fed him every day at one o'clock. The children who played in the churchyard, the only green spot in the neighbourhood, knew and loved Bobby. The faithful little dog lived like this, never more than a stone's throw from the grave, for nine years.

Then, suddenly, over-zealous officials began to ask

questions. Who did Bobby belong to? Where was his collar? Who paid for his dog licence – or hadn't he got one? Mr Traill was accused of encouraging stray dogs, and Bobby was ordered to be destroyed.

Greyfriars Bobby

There was a great protest, from all the children who played in the churchyard, and the case came to the ears of Edinburgh's Lord Provost. He declared that in future he himself would pay Bobby's licence every year, and he bought a collar for him. The inscription ran 'Greyfriars Bobby from the Lord Provost – licensed', and today the collar, and the feeding bowl Bobby used at Traill's Dining Rooms, are on show in one of Edinburgh's Museums.

For Bobby had become famous – in his last years he was one of the sights of Edinburgh, and when he died at last, after keeping his faithful watch over Old Jock's grave for fourteen years, the statue with a drinking fountain was put up to his memory.

The music of Scotland

Near the statue there's a pub called 'Bobby's Tavern'. There are taverns all over Edinburgh, and they all have one thing in common – a great row of bottles of different kinds of whisky. I had never imagined there were so many varieties.

But not only do the Scots drink Scotch whisky, it is Scotland's chief export. Last year they sent seventy million gallons out of the country – five hundred and sixty million bottles. To the Scot it is the Water of Life, or as they say in the Gaelic 'Uisghe beathe'. It is what wine is to the French, and it is with whisky that the famous toast 'The Immortal Memory' is drunk to Scotland's most famous poet, Robert Burns.

Burns is the man who can still strike a spark in the heart of every Scotsman. He was born in 1756 and his family were small farmers. His early years were spent in poverty, but he learnt to read, and was a passionate compulsive reader of every book that came his way, particularly verses and old ballads. He learned them by heart, and sang them when he was out in the fields.

Then he began to write verses of his own – and what verses!

It was in Edinburgh that his greatness was recognized and established. Edinburgh loved Burns, and Burns loved Edinburgh – All the Gay World he called it.

Burns' life work was devoted to the songs of Scotland, finding the half-forgotten songs of the countryside, writing them down, and saving them for Scotsmen down the centuries. 'Caledonia's Bard', he was proclaimed; Robert Burns, who gave the world 'Auld Lang Syne'.

But other music is played in Edinburgh, especially at the time of the Edinburgh Festival.

The Edinburgh Festival of Music and Arts, lasting three weeks, every August and September, was started just after the Second World War. It brings to Scotland's capital the best orchestras, musicians, conductors, singers, dancers of the day, as well as new plays and great actors. Another movement has developed in the shadow of the festival – called the fringe. Here events which are youthful, experimental and sometimes disrespectful also get a showing.

But in spite of this galaxy of international culture and new thinking, throughout the festival the greatest, the most popular, the most sold-out attraction, remains obstinately Scottish and traditional: the Floodlit Tattoo on the Esplanade of the Castle.

At night, with its floodlighting, the castle seems like a fairy castle floating above Princes Street. Along the esplanade the Scottish regiments dance and the pipes play tunes that Scottish regiments have danced and marched to for centuries past. Tunes with titles like

'Scotland the Brave', 'The Black Bear', 'The Nut Brown Maiden'.

A Piper

Halfway down the Royal Mile there's a little green-painted shop with a set of bagpipes in the window; over the door is a sign that reads ' J. & R. Glen – Bagpipe makers'. I went inside and asked a man with a kilt and a large brown beard if they still made bagpipes on the premises. ' Go through into the workshop and speak to my father,' he said. 'He knows more about it than me. I've only been in the trade for twenty-five years. He's been at it for nearly sixty!'

I walked through, as 'young' Mr Ross suggested, towards the sound of the whirring lathe. The workshop was a tiny, dark room powdered with white dust blowing from the workbench. Shelves around the walls were piled high with chanters and mouth pieces and drones. Some looked as if they had been there for hundreds of years. In fact, the whole room had a weird quality, like a film set for a Dickensian sweat-shop. I couldn't make out Mr Ross at first, and then a small gnome-like figure turned round from the lathe where he was working.

He was wearing a black Homburg hat, and a long fawn overall that almost reached to the floor. His hat and overall and glasses and eyebrows were completely covered in white fluff which I afterwards learned were shavings from an ivory mouthpiece that he had just been turning. He looked as if he'd just come in out of a snowstorm.

'Just feel how smooth this is,' he said. 'It's modern art ivory, which is impervious to damp – an important thing – and to heat as well.' I asked if he always used ivory.

'Ivory, ebony, African blackwood and Cuban caucus. There'll be no more Cuban caucus, though – it's all been cut down. That's the last up there on the shelf, broken out in 1896.'

'Broken out?' I queried.

'Aye. For the chanter we make a quick tapered bore, roughly seven-eighths of an inch at the bottom and one-eighth at the top. Then we say it's broken out, and it lies on the shelf up there. The longer it lies the better. We used to keep the Cuban caucus wood for the gold-mounted pipes. The Indian Rajahs, you know, were the only people stupid enough to pay money for gold mounted pipes.'

I asked him when bagpipes were first invented.

'Oh, the pipes were made in ancient China, 4,500 years ago. But they didn't have a bag, d'ye see! I could never understand why the Chinese – so clever in many ways – never thought of adding a bag!'

'Who were the first people to use a bag?' I asked.

'I think it was the Turks. The Indians used a gourd, but it wasn't a proper inflatable bag. But the Turks were very keen on martial music and marching. I think it was them who really started the bag. And then it spread all over Europe – Russia, Bulgaria, Yugoslavia, Spain, Germany.'

'So bagpipes are all over the world?'

'Aye. But no one has brought them to such a standard of perfection as the Highland pipes.'

I asked him if he knew why the pipes had caught on so well in Scotland.

'Ah, well, d'ye see, there used to be a good deal of marching and fighting in Scotland. And a Scotsman will march for miles behind the pipes and drums. And there's none so fearless as a Scotsman in battle when he hears the skirl of the pipes. The Scots are a very emotional people, too, and the pipes can be used for every emotional circumstance, from the charge to the lament. And

There's nae instrument, however sweet,
Can with the Highland pipes compete.'

Just across the High Street from this incredible shop is St Giles' Cathedral, and in it there's a special little chapel of the Most Ancient and Most Noble Order of the Thistle, the highest order of Scottish chivalry. In the roof, among amazingly rich carving, there are cherubs playing all sorts of musical instruments. And one cherub is playing the bagpipes.

For – as the man who carved it said – 'There must be *one* Scotsman somewhere in Heaven!'